BIG COCKS

Hilarious Snaps of Prominent Poultry

summersdale

CHARLIE ELLIS

BIG COCKS

An Hachette UK Company
www.hachette.co.uk

Summersdale Publishers Ltd
Part of Octopus Publishing Group Limited
Carmelite House
50 Victoria Embankment
LONDON
EC4Y 0DZ
UK

www.summersdale.com

Printed and bound in China

ISBN: 978-1-80007-008-0

To..................................

From...........................

Why the f•ck do you think I crossed the road?

BEING AN "EARLY RISER"
ISN'T ALWAYS A BAD THING.

Chicks love it when I make it stand all the way up.

JAIL BIRD

I THINK YOU'LL FIND *MINE'S* BIGGER THAN *YOURS*.

Are you egging me on, ladies?

Who you calling a chicken? Oh yeah, right... never mind.

A CHICKEN AND AN EGG WALK INTO A BAR. THE BARTENDER SAYS, "WHO'S FIRST?"

How much more noise
do I need to make to
get some attention
around here?

What do you call a confident chicken? Cocky.

THE COCK MAKING ALL THAT NOISE EARLIER WENT THATAWAY!

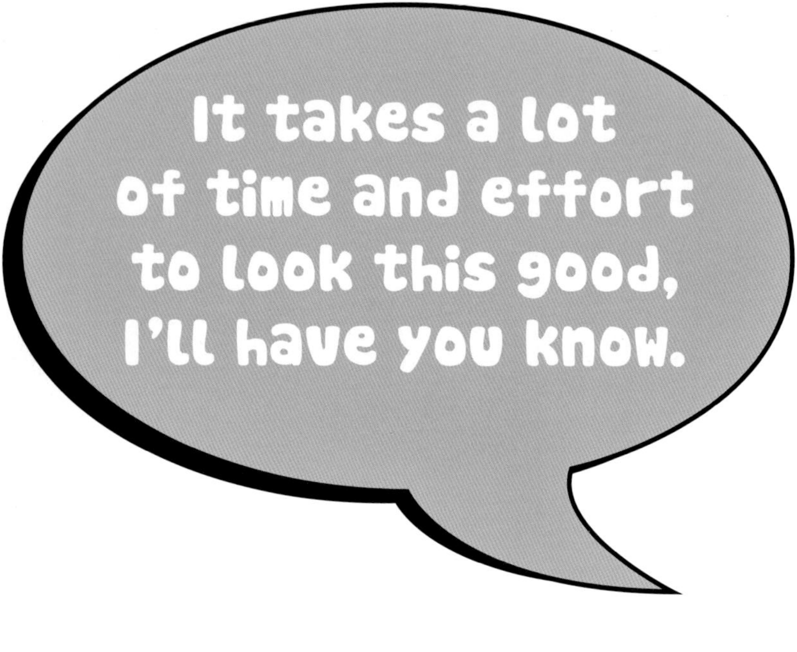
It takes a lot of time and effort to look this good, I'll have you know.

WHAT ARE YOU LOOKING AT, MOTHERCLUCKER?

When the bassline drops...

ONE SMALL STEP FOR MAN.
ONE GIANT LEAP FOR COCK-KIND.

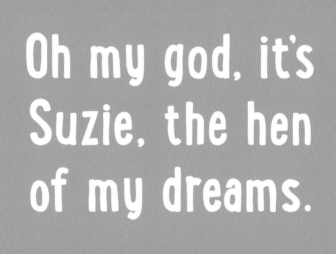

Oh my god, it's Suzie, the hen of my dreams.

If you like it fast,
I'm your cock.
#QUICKCOCK

SOME SAY I'M A PUNK, BUT I'M JUST A LITTLE ANAR-COCK.

I CALL THIS ONE
"STANDING TO ATTENTION"!

I am a big
pecker, yes.

YOU'VE HEARD THE TERM COCK
OF THE WALK? I'M THE COCK
AND THIS IS THE WALK.

Nothing like waking up to a big cock.

No shade intended, but I'm the biggest cock around here.

IMAGE CREDITS

If you're interested in finding out more about our books, find us on Facebook at **Summersdale Publishers**, on Twitter at **@Summersdale** and on Instagram at **@summersdalebooks**.

www.summersdale.com